The Keys to Success and Wealth

Law of Attraction

Arsenio R. Pelayo

Chapter One

A detailed deep examination

of

Law of Attraction

Chapter Two

Wealth Affirmation

Law of attraction is the keys to success and wealth. The ability to pull to you almost anything that you can visualize and make a feeling in order to get a good grip of this concept. Step one, understanding the universal law, creating miracles in your life is no more complicated than understanding the metaphysics of the universal though and because that law is basically indestructible and therefore infinite, we know that the power used by miracle makers in the past is still available today yet to non Muslim society where brought up to believe only in those things that we can logically understand. We are not told either that the universal law has limited potential or that this power is that Todd disposal. It can be used to what? Miracles, you know, own lives. To understand miracles, we have to look at two aspects of the universal. Firstly, there lies deep within all mankind and immense power and secondly that power is impartial and unemotional.

The universal mind or Christ consciousness on what to will and does this power that allows man in recognition of the universal life force that we call God the life force. It's a tunnel. It is a part of all things. It is a major part of each of us. Consequently, we all have within us and unlimited power. Creating miracles in our lives becomes a matter of identifying with the power and understanding its characteristics and learning to use it effectively. This identification achieve by knowing that the power is within you and acknowledging that fact by saying, I'm eternal, immortal, universal, and infinite and what I am is beautiful and this manner. You look into the past and you're poised for the next step, which involves looking at its characteristics. The universal flow is impartial and unemotional. It has no way of knowing what you want. Noah does it discriminate between your hopes and aspirations, likes and dislikes.

It is pure energy and accepts whatever thoughts, feelings, and actions you project and reflects them back to you and emotionally in the form of events that you experience day to day. It must the same way as that electricity illuminates both abrupt. I'm the biggest teapot. The universal law does not differentiate between different types of energy in your life. It will give you anything you believe in. No more I no less. Therefore, the key to understanding miracles is so look at the beliefs you express as thoughts and feelings when you are born, your thoughts and feelings are limitless because your mind does a clean slate. What the small child protects into the universe. Law is a natural purity unbounded by the constraints of beliefs. Children often attempt the seemingly impossible other way that they have any physical limitations. They drive up in the family car or walking a high ledge and it's only later for education that they learn the confines of human expectancy, but these confines of boundaries, how illusions they are formed by belief patterns.

Most of them born of ignorance handed down from generation to generation. This pool of belief patterns or collective unconscious as call you called, it gains validity as it moves through time and eventually the concepts that the later generation experiences as physical reality become rigid and domineering. It is as billions of people who proceeded. You have determined what you're going to experience on the palladium and that is all that there is to it and weekend into does nothing allow for genius or for the understanding that we're now in an era of rapid enfoldment. Fundamental structures are being swept away and an avalanche of awareness and we are no longer prepared just to read about great miracle makers. We want to have the same experience for most people. This is not possible because they are locked within the limitations of body and mind. Their upbringing is so dominant that didn't cases then tie but I may spirits little spiritual growth.

Step two, understanding life's mission. We are not taught bodies or our emotions online, so any of the structures and restrictions we experienced around us. We have an infinite pod. The God force using the physical form to experience spiritual development to a special training called daily life. When you went to the earth plane, the energy that is the real and you left, it's a boat in the higher consciousness of pure light and then took by choice the body you are now in. You chose the circumstances of this life because it was the next step in your infinite evolution and because this life would allow you to expand what through all spiritually so that you could become an even greater expression of the infinite life force, all living spirit. Now you may say, that's nuts. Why would I choose these circumstances of my life, this family, this society, and this neighborhood?

Why did I not choose a more affluent environment or put pretty up on a more intellectual capacity? The onset lies in that dimension beyond the physical plane. As you enter this dimension pooper you had within your consciousness, I had road commission at go. The nature of that goal is foam. The Whitten in the very deepest recesses of the you know you and want to out today, no matter what to feel about yourself are actually a part of that goal and its various stages of completion. You'll mind began recording events, thoughts and feelings. Only at birth it does not know of you. How right mission Nolan, does it understand the universal law that interacts with your limitless potential. Why? Two reasons. First, if your mind, feelings and emotions knew the nature of your heroic Golan life, there'll be no challenge or quest and your evolution would suffer.

Secondly, most understanding of metaphysics is based on tribal or religious beliefs which do not totally reflect an accurate perception of the delicacy of energy and the way its ebbs and flows affect daily life. No real understanding of the universal law has ever been incorporated into the various belief patterns of the well's collective unconscious. For example, that is say that your heroic goal in life is to learn to love yourself and to accept full cosmic responsibility for what you are and let us say you've had a number of previous experiences on the earth plane in which you were wheat can indulge yourself metaphysically by leaning on others rather than contributing to your own energy or support. If you knew of this in advance, you would begin to favor one course of action over another. You would intellectualize yourself into positions or feelings that you wanted to achieve and your mind would dominate your every move.

Evolution does not work that way. You cannot
overcome weakness by fighting it or thinking your
way out of it. You can overcome weakness by
leaving it behind. This means that you become
aware of the inner tendencies that bring you
down, that do not support the belief in itself, that
do not until us a love of self and you say, I don't
want to be that anymore. Then you move yourself
out of the Slovenly ways of the collective
unconscious into discipline and power. From time
to time you may drift back, but once you decide
on the side of strength, the pile of the universal
low wind always is with you to varying degrees. It
may be a battle at first because your mind does
not understand these laws or the nature of Gil.
Michelle. On that note, does it understand the
laws that govern new potential?

It'll have a tendency to advise you logically from its own experience and logic is death to that pub view. That is a miracle maker. Step free, understanding the nature of beliefs. The next step in creating your own miracles is to look at the nature of beliefs by reviewing beliefs and feelings. You begin to understand how to use the universal law effectively. It is natural to young for the impossible and in so doing, you establish strong beliefs about what can and cannot be done. You can jump a seven high to no higher run at a sudden speed. I know faster except a sudden position. I know better. It because commercial air crosses flies at about 600 miles an hour. The short this time in which you can get from New York to Paris is about six hours. Those are the facts in the collective unconscious. But what if I told you of a man who could move his body many thousands of miles in just a few seconds, your mind would scan his memory banks and drew a blank, whereupon you might think impossible.

Then perhaps you might review all the scientific data available and conclude that this feed is unachievable well as scientific knowledge and current thinking of products at the same collective unconscious and just the fact that a billion people have no concept of a man moving 3000 miles in a few seconds makes it impossible. But the billions of people along there are not. I mentioned right here on the earth plane and which such a fetus possible and there were a few people alive today who know of this dimension and use it. It is a matter of perception than belief. Your ability to work miracles is predicated entirely on how easily and quickly you can give the collective unconscious. The slip is your attachment to the collective unconscious or weld belief patterns that hold you back. This attachment which you accepted at birth is your main challenge in life and your spiritual goal is to step above it.

Eventually you realize that in order to become a part of a higher consciousness, you have to leave where you are right now and step into the unknown. That is why all the tales of the path of the initiates talk about loneliness for as you move away from the old energy, there's a sense of loss. As you take that step, you'll perception expand gradually to accept a high up vibration of self and you understand what others believe as a part of their evolution, but it's not the sum total of all of the facts. We experience life through the five senses, the windows of the soul, and we had taught what capacity those senses have. Yet each of them has a dimension that is many times deeper than is normally perceived and those dimensions will open for you as you move towards that is liquid feelings, true feelings.

Eventually you realize that in order to become a part of a higher consciousness, you have to leave where you are right now and step into the unknown. That is why all the tales of the path of the initiates talk about loneliness for as you move away from the old energy, there's a sense of loss. As you take that step, you'll perception expand gradually to accept a high up vibration of self and you understand what others believe as a part of their evolution, but it's not the sum total of all of the facts. We experience life through the five senses, the windows of the soul, and we had taught what capacity those senses have. Yet each of them has a dimension that is many times deeper than is normally perceived and those dimensions will open for you as you move towards that is liquid feelings, true feelings.

You can enter into other worlds and press interest in this. A hype and sense of feeling is a capacity you can learn to develop quite quickly. You can enter into areas of perception that few people ever experience. Everything around you is energy, your body, its various organs, your thoughts, the physical place you inhabit, the events of your life. Each expresses an energy, a positive. That energy is perceivable through the five senses, but most of it is beyond normal perception. By opening to the pile of the universal law and controlling the mind who centering. Anticipate. You become aware of the subtlety of energies around you will find that you can use your feelings to guide you through life. As you move into a situation, push your feelings into what type of lies ahead.

How does it feel? What are the universal laws
saying to which areas flow and which do not.
After a while, this exercise becomes simple and
very accurate. You may not be able to see all the
subtle energies around, but you can learn to feel
them as soon you will find the information from
universal has a way of jumping at you.
Unexpected events in your lives. Gather energy as
they come towards you and you can feel that
energy, weeks and even years before they occur.
Signs will tell you that are not possible to precede
the future. And that is true for those who believe
it's so. But as you move out to the worlds group
perception feeling and even seeing the future will
become second nature to you to honestly universal
effectively you should watch this manifestation,
which is basically every event in your life than
linkage event to underlying feelings and attitude.

We realize that when things go well, it is solely because you put that image into the universal law and it responded. Imagine the universal law as a shipping clerk in a large mail order company. He gets your old up that has no idea who you are. If the order says size eight he sends out size eight it is of no concern to him whether or not size eight fits your humanity complies with your request in daily life, your feelings, thoughts and attitudes so before you decide to change your present conditions, you have to be very sure what you want from life. That universal law, we act specifically to onset messages. You have to ride clearly and you have to be able to accept whatever you're looking for that let's say you want to win a large sum of money. Give up your job and spend the rest of your days lying in the sun.

You dream about the cash and you sign and you say, wouldn't it be lovely, but is that actually what you want? You might very soon find yourself bored and video mind would like to lounge in the sun. Being a, you might say, I should've stayed well was there was more potential than creating energy for yourself. The universal goal is not just a matter of wishing for things Willy Nelly. You have to realize that the power is within you and once you take the first step towards it, whatever you create will be fail highest good. It might not be exactly what you thought you wanted, but you had better. Be ready for the consequences before embarking on a miracle action plan. You ought to spend some time meditating on the conditions, on material objects you want. The universal law is the shipping clock waiting for your clear and concise order.

The currencies with which you're going to pay for. It is belief to create something with absolute certainty. You have to establish the feeling within you that it has already happened, that the condition you desire is already a part of your life that can be hot because your mind knowing nothing about the workings of the lobe fights back. You have, um, I am witch and your mind contradicts, you know, not that conflict that developed confused as the universal law, which is about to deliver your heart's desire. This clash of opposing energies has been the challenge of the initiative since the beginning of time. It is the hunt for the Holy Grail. Well, the slaying of the Dragon. It states that no one end is the Kingdom of heaven with him until he has tamed the Dragon of negativity that he inherited from the collective unconscious.

Figuratively, you will have to leave the earth plane even though you may be still very much a part of physical reality dimensions and not out there as something that is between you and the stars there. You know quotes already not chucks. These journeys have an inner reality and an outer manifestation in the physical, so anything you can conceive is actually a part of you right now. The fact that you do not have it to hand Matt does not. Whatever it is that you can see is in a state of gradual becoming. If you'll phone I am, which you have to start feeling rich, thinking rich and holding a rich attitude. Walk around expensive stores have coffee and the best hotel in town begin to act and feel as if you already have good fortune. You know the universe up to deliver to you.

You create a concrete reality of wealth within
your inner journey and it will then become
manifest in your outer chatty the physical world.
If you can maintain that feeling of power and live
as if your wish has already been granted by the
universal goal, you'll wish will be delivered
guaranteed, but you cannot be half hearted or you
will dissipate your personal power and nothing
will happen. You'll have to take the puff like a
warrior. You're going to achieve your goal no
matter what. Convince you no matter where you
are right now no matter what adversity face you;
you will reach your objective. Universal law does
not care whether you have your heart's desire or
not. Therefore, you might as well make up your
mind to collect.

You can have anything you want and when you create it, it becomes yours. Often we feel we do not deserve success or wealth or complete health or anything else we might we have told to in childhood that we're not worthy or that somehow we owe something to society or the physical plane or that we have some kind of special sin that we should have tone full before we can enjoy what we want type of life. That is not the case. The law does not discriminate. It receives your energy and delivers diamonds or plain rocks. Depending on what you printed, it is very important to look at the negative feelings you have about yourself. It is easy to say, oh, I never win anything or I'm too old. They will never hire me all. I can never be with that person. I'm not pretty enough. That kind of thinking is indicative of the mind and its logical advice.

Miracles, I'm not logical. So the last thing you need is logical advice from the mind. Women such advice has given, acknowledged the mind, thank it and say I do not accept any energy that is contrary to the unlimited power that lies within me. Then press on. Infinite power is so McManus, so powerful, so much more than the mind that it exists in a separate dimension and that is why the mind has difficulty perceiving that it is. Even that you will get an intuitional feeling or a rescue excitement. But that is all. You cannot really hear it, touch it or taste it, but it comes around the mind like a breeze. And when it stops to what can your life, you will know it by the quality of the people and the events that surround you. Before we go to step forward, the Miracle Action Plan that just briefly review some important points. The universal or living spirit is unlimited. Therefore, what do you offer is unlimited?

The universal law is impartial and unemotional. It cannot discriminate. It will give you anything you believe in. You are not your body or your emotions or your mind. You are part of the living spirit learning. No matter what your circumstance is, the universal law can be called upon at any time because it is the real you. Whatever you create for yourself by understanding the mystical metaphysical aspects of the universal goal is yours because you created it. You deserve it. Miracles are not kissing from God. They are part of you which has got finally the universal law is in balance and harmony by its very nature and so as you set out on your action plan, you will not be able to infringe on habits. Whatever you create will have to be for yourself. You cannot will the universal law onto out this by saying; I want this to happen to my friend.

This would be infringing because not knowing the nature of your friends, heroic life plan, you are not entitled to change it when any way old to what he is going through at this time. He has to expand his life for himself as he also has unlimited power within him and a part of his growth pattern is discovering that fact. Within the universal law there is no dual energy. One power that pervades so will things and everything is a pot on that power differentiation between good and evil is just your perception for within real energy there is no judgment. There is high energy and not so high in the g and at the end of this life you will have the opportunity to review what to have achieved which will be a matter of how much you've succeeded in centering your life in a discipline of perceiving that living spirit and using it, but your review will not to be emotional.

You'd be looking at the quality or speed if you're like of the energy you created. If you have harmed others, you have impeded your evolution by decelerating the life force within you. That is your comic energy and someday you would have to understand that it was not too high as pop, but you cannot judge others because since the energy your mind perceives does not to cooperate the nature of the heroic goal, you have no way of knowing exactly what they need comically for that growth. At this infinite point in that evolution, there are no accidents or victims. Each person who's responsible please own evolution. Each pulls to themselves the circumstances experienced in life. He puts in that in the oldest so to speak and gets back tweed cracked cups that is upon the learning pattern, trial and error.

This lifetime is yours. You may be involved in relationships and loved ones, but basically what you make up your life and how you pass through it is your evolution. We all learn to take responsibility, phones, circumstances, and within the universal law you're not expected to take responsibility for the evolution of others. It sound a bit harsh, but in the law there's an incredible clarity and justice. That is why adversity is so useful. It allows people to look for something beyond day to day reality and this brings them in touch with their true inner selves. In desperation, they begin to put on that unlimited power and they realize that anything can be changed and suffering.

It has been said that they'll no incurable diseases, only incurable people, and that is true of all energy within the universal though trying to fix your circumstances just physically or mentally will not work in the long run because deep rooted in consistencies will continue to surface in your life in various disguises to overcome something once. If a world means going within yourself to discover the real cause of the disturbance, this process or discovery will allow you more energy which you can use to create the things you want in life. Step full, the Miracle Action Plan. Write down on a piece of paper and it would have been pulled in this those things in the conditions you want.

Do not let the mind advice you. It has limitations. Shoot for the moon. I'd be sure you leave nothing out Trump and change your list until you're comfortable with it. But be clear about what you want. Using sacked and precise wording to describe the conditions you require. Remember the system works so you must be definite in the way you described your once his what to do a read them as three times a day once when you rise once in the middle of the day and once before bed. He made it meditate on your miracles from time to time and know that the universal laws received award and is just about to deliver. Talking about your miracle dissipates the energy trust. Think about your miracles as though you already have the conditions you desire.

Page 28

Your heart's desire can come from anywhere. Do
not limit your field of expectation. Remain open
and flexible at all time and smile a lot. The first
miracle is on its way. Step five, understanding
energy. Since the mind has no way of knowing
how the universal law has gone to tribal miracle,
do not waste your time trying to figure out. Just
know your thoughts should be like acorns that
develop gradually into oaks. If you dig them up to
discover how things are going, your tree will
perish. It is important to avoid fretting sent to
them the feeling that some way somehow the
universal law would not let you down because
everything in the universe is energy.

Atoms and molecules move at the speed of light. In fact, reality is about solid and not solid at the same time, and this applies to pulled forms. They are real and even more powerful than physical reality because they're not constrained by the limits of the material plane. You cannot take them apart and analyze them. You have to create them and let them fly. Enthusiasm and belief. You energize a universal law and encourage it to deliver. Tried to keep your thoughts pure and on target. If doubt creeps in, do not allow it to dominate. Look at doubt from above yourself. Realize that it is just the mind set of not understanding. Creating objections through ignorance and whatever you have set in motion will happen. As you work with a pot. It'll have a way of showing you the next move at every.

Know that this inner force is so powerful that it
pulls you into excitement and adventure beyond
your dreams. Keep it pure, remained silent, and
remember to keep your methods secret.
Everything that surrounds you has the living spirit
within it in varying degrees living things express
it more than do inanimate objects. The more you
come in touch with the universal though within
you, the more you're in touch with things around.
Everything becomes a symbol and strength to
you. The world helps you and the fuller you
become, the more dimensions you can pull from.
A very dear friend was walking along the street
one day wondering what to do with her life. She
was at the crossroads literally and figuratively.
Life was flat.

She craved inspiration. As she stepped from the curb, I nearly knocked her over and as it's creased round the corner, a book fell out of the trunk. It was a book about man's quest for the universal power and it changed her life shortly. She left the town and then bumped in a whole new evolutionary path that over a period of time has taken it to great metaphysical heights and into countries and relationships she could not have conceived of before. The universal low provided her with a special teaching in the form of that book and she being into was ready to benefit and so it should be for you as you work towards your miracle, watch for every sign, for every change around her and you will see the universal communicating with you.

The more you trusted, the more the energy is encourage to reveal itself and various unusual things begin to occur. Your energy quickens and opportunities pop up like colts on a lake, then you will know that the power is truly with you. This coming into more than anything else will help you manifest your desires. You cannot act negatively in one part of the unit bustle. I expect the other pods to deliver your miracles unaffected. As you want your life you become expert reading symbols and you see that you are the only one responsible for what you are and that everything around you expresses an energy. The clothes you wear, the things you say, the people you associate with, the food you eat, the places you go.

Old State comes to the universal law of what you are. The quality of these statements or the coming in tune with yourself and your surroundings is the key to your spiritual enfoldment. What you are has great power. Its energy oscillates and reflects the amount of living spirit or God false that you express. The more you work on your life, the more you accept responsibility, the more energy you will have and the greater will be when you look at it as energy and you understand the laws of attraction, you're basically pulling to you. There was all that you need through a dimension that is not solid. If you see a body to solid, I see the circumstances around you as solid.

It somewhat limits your ability to believe in it happening, and so I felt it was an important point to begin to establish this idea of you have consciousness you can create through the pop your fault. If your life force and your strength are strong, you can more or less materialize things instantaneously. If it is not so strong, it'll take time, but you'll thinking in terms of something coming towards you in a sea of energy law other than through the fragmented and more obscure logical process where often there isn't a logical explanation as to how things actually work. I think of your energy as you begin to develop into this miracle maker is that you should consider detaching somewhat from the social, ethnic, tribal energy that we all come from.

We were all born somewhere. We will born a part
of one tribe or another that the tribe may now
have expanded to 50 million people, but it's still a
tribe. It's a mindset. It's a socio economic unit, and
as you pull out of that a little bit, it allows you the
freedom to isolate, foster, to vibrate foster. If you
are much sucked into the old tribal ways, then
what happens is you take on the identity of the
tribe rather than an identity of yourself. So let's
say for example, you're Irish, you can love Ireland
and you can read the Irish poets and you can
recall the times that you had. But within your Irish
race, you have to bring that back inside of
yourself and say, I am an individual. The fact that
I was born in Ireland was a factor of my
evolution, but first I met individually.

Secondly, Irishman and as you begin to detach
one pace of one step away from the tribal energy,
then again, you begin to win back your power.
You begin to win back that power that will create
the miracles for you throughout the whole of time
and throughout the history of man's struggle
within himself that have been, that initiates, that
have been great beings that have managed to go
beyond the limitations of the earth plane and they
way they did it was they won the battle of the
mind. There's a part of you that will hold onto the
negativity, the fragmented, the ego, the belief in
limitation and is upon a view that is expansive and
loving and joyous and heading out, and those two
pots will always be in contention with each other
at the beginning.

Perhaps the negative pots, all of the personality part may maybe much; much stronger than the positive expansive part of you and the name of the game is to begin to overwhelm the negativity with positivity. You've heard me talk perhaps in the past about being careful with your vocabulary, being careful with the way that you present yourself. If you're going to come out of positivity, you have to come out of it all of the time. You have to establish that energy inside of you and energy of hope, one of transcendence, one of serving humanity without infringing upon them, and then as you begin to do that, the inner mind that it pertains so much of that negativity, that darkness, it begins to back away.

But you have to remember that you've been on the earth plane a certain amount of years and that in a mind is not going to let go just because you say get out of it. It has dominated the in a mind that negativity of the in the mind. It has control of your life, where weed has had control of your life. Often it'll make you sick, it'll make your body sick just to control you. It'll cause difficulty just to be able to feel that it is in control. As you begin to become more infinite, the ego or the dog part of the mind begins to back off and you may have a feeling that you are dying. And of course that is a natural feeding on the pile and it isn't your physical death that you are looking at.

What you're looking at is that the personality is giving ground to the infinity and so the personality will have a feeling of its losing importance or dying. As you push out as a miracle maker and as you begin to get this action plan going, you have to establish in your feelings the idea that one you are worthy to, you can receive. So often our society, we put an emphasis on giving. That is more blessing to give than to receive. But you have to understand for every giver that has to be a receiver. When you feel comfortable in receiving, when a person offers you something, take it.

It doesn't matter if you don't want it because sure enough, if it becomes a part of your possessions in that kind of energy. Begin to practice accepting and you see money in the street, pick it up. We're supposed to concentrate on, first of all, I've got outside of ourselves and secondarily people in the society that was supposed to assist or aid in some way. The philosophy that I teach is one way you turn and you face yourself understanding that if you become strong, then you have a gift that you can take to society. So many people I meet as I travel and do seminars in the Pacific and all over the world. They want to serve humanity, they want to give and yet they don't really have any true power with which to give.

They want to assist the world to go beyond poverty but they don't have any money themselves. They want to heal the world. But they bought me sick. And so as you are looking at that, you understand that you're on your own. Well one of that is to reflect you back to yourself. That is his function and that's the function of interpersonal relationships. They out there so you learn about yourself and in fact you are an individual evolving through the physical plane and that individuality is sacrosanct. Then you have to make it important, and I don't mean it in an ego sense of the word, but you remember that you are on your own.

You come in as an individual and you go out as an individual. You remember in the book goals, so I said the universe little has no way of knowing what that is. You want that. Sometimes it's confusing for people because they think in terms of God being all knowing and the way that I would like to explain it to you for your consideration is this, whereas the gold falls or the life force is in all things, which is true. It does not have a concentration minute by minute on each individual part. It would be the same as if you owned or were president of a huge multinational corporation. You may know that you have a branch in Nigeria but you don't know at 9:00 AM on Tuesday whether the secretary is off sick or not or whether the electricity has blown a fuse on the telex isn't working or whatever it may be. You're not intimately emotionally involved in the day by day.

That's how you're controlling the situational. That is how you are allowing this corporation to evolve the life force being in all things, not having an opinion. Being impartial is not involved in knowing what you want or having a decision. It is not as if God says for you to be rich as good for you to be poor is bad. God doesn't say we want you to be healthy and it doesn't say it's bad to be sick. It doesn't have an opinion. And if you think about it, that idea sets you free because once it doesn't have an opinion; it can reflect back to you exactly what you are with an uninterrupted and totally pure reflection. You don't want to reflection coming back to you that has somebody's opinion in it because you'd be heading off to the beach and the opinion might say go to the concert if you know what I mean.

And so when you understand that, you have to be very clear about what it is you want and what you're putting into the universe. A little as you look at your Miracle Action Plan, you can't be wishy washy. If you just put in an affirmation that says, I want more money, what does that mean? If you're in confusion, if you have a certain amount of indecision about what your heroic life's goal is or what your mission in life is, then you need to begin to get back inside of yourself and clear. And sometimes that may take months, but that's okay. You have plenty of time and as you uncomplicated your life and you move towards simplicity up from within, you naturally comes, hey, I want to be a violinist. Hey, what I really want to do is go and live on a farm in North Africa or whatever it might be. The key to that miracle making process is balance.

Without balance, you really don't have a chance because, once you're trying to do as this, you're trying to use the infinity of the lie to know things to carry to you, the result that you want and because the light comes out of purity and balance, it can only be congruent with you if you are balanced and balanced means a balanced physical situation. You don't have to heal everything going on in your body, but at least it has to be balanced and you'd have to love yourself by caring for your physical body, working on it, being aware when things go wrong, being aware of putting in the correcting action, going off and studying and knowing about your body.

And then the second point of balance of course, is emotional, which we had talked about in the past, and then the mental balance is understanding that for the miracles to happen, you can't engage too much logic otherwise you'd destroy your belief in the medical showing up and between those three items of physical violence, emotional balance and mental balance, you walk through the physical plane in a measured and powerful way. You don't rush. You don't allow yourself to get out of control. You don't give away your power unless you particularly have to upon this. You make it your own decision to do so and you tried to keep as much of your life as immaculate as possible.

Then as you begin to create this action plan and you begin to put those miracles up in your mind, you're going to have to remember that there is no time because we live in a state of the tunnel now and in that heat tonal now you have to create your affirmation, your visualization or your goal in your feelings. If you can feel it grunted if you can feel yourself moving through those circumstances that you designed so much, they will be they. If you think that they are outside of you or that they were attainable at a later date than that, you'll never pull to you those things that you want and then as you became to resonate those feelings and you begin to nudge up as little flame of your own intention.

Then because it is within you and because you believe it, it is grounded but there was a time lag between you conceptualizing the feeling, conceptualizing the goal of the miracle production plan and when it is delivered, I didn't that time you are going to have to be patient. No negative yearning, no frustration, no stumping you foot, whatever. You have to wait and the more you wait and you know it will be that. That in itself becomes an affirmation where you pull it to you 10 years in the life of a human being is not a long time.

It seems long because we live in minute by minute, hour by hour, day by day, but 10 years is not a long time and so as you put out those ideas, you wait any kind of negativity, any emotion, any negative yearning, and you destroy the planet as you begin to change yourself into this exhilarating, exciting, fluid, adventure seeking person. I like the use of affirmations and affirmations or words that you invent or words that you particularly like that means something special to you that for them you'll individuality, your power, your strength. For example, the first affirmation in the miracles book that I read out to you was positive individual.

You're affirming that the power lies with you. I'm not with somebody else. You affirming that there's a positivity and goodness on how road is in that power and then you're looking at the day and you're saying whatever happens is a part of my greater evolution. I'm not so intimately involved in the emotion of what's going on. I understand that all of it is for my highest good and as you begin to create that kind of affirmation within yourself and you repeat them from time to time, what happens is that the contents of your mind changes then wanted reflects out into life changes and the quality of your life improves.

The last part of this that we need to consider is the concept of creative visualization. Creative visualization really means the ability to use your imagination to stimulate your feelings into believing that the situation is so before it actually materializes in your life. Because, you've probably heard me say before, the inner mind does not know the difference between fact and fantasy. Creative visualization is a powerful tool that you can use for yourself. Some people have difficulty using their imagination, they have difficulty. You visualizing events or visualizing dream sequences and that is a habit that you have to fold in for yourself using your imagination, using your ability to fantasize.

Using your ability to see things in the mind's eye increases your ability to affect events in the world because not only can you develop other possibilities, more limitless possibilities perhaps, but also once you can see yourself walking through as seen, you can be a pontificate through the laws of attraction. What comes to you will flick that in an energy that you hold, what you've been taking, and the energy that you've created in your life so far. And so imagine this, if you can create a powerful and strong image of yourself as a miracle maker, as this wonderful, wonderful human being that has so much to give, so much to offer the world, then that being comes alive. It is almost as if by putting that energy into the mind, you shine a light in there that stimulates the mind.

And so whereas often people have moved so far away from fantasy and imagination and so suddenly into materialism of logic that they don't have an ability to conceptualize things that are not actually logically right there in front of them. They don't have the ability unless they can literally touch it and taste it and see it. If you can begin to practice this idea of creating your imagination the way that you want to see yourself, then you have within you a wonderful tool that will allow you to become a more powerful be. You can use creative visualization for self-acceptance and that in itself is a very large project.

For some people do you accept yourself the way
you are? Do you accept, for example, the shape of
your face you'll face is whatever shape you've
created it, what images shape it came out as so to
speak, and you have to see that shape as beautiful.
You have to be able to stand in the mirror, in the
bathroom naked and say with all sincerity, this is
utter beauty and once you can see that beautiful, it
becomes more beautiful. Once it becomes more
beautiful to say this is out, the beauty becomes
simpler and so first of all, you can look at the
whole concept of self acceptance. If you will give
yourself time to go beyond your limitations. If
you will forgive yourself for those parts of
yourself that are less than powerful or less than
honorable, then you begin to heal your entire
personality.

There's nothing worse than meeting a person that has a tremendously fragmented personality, full of guilt trips, full of negativity, full of lack of self image. What's nice about two ways that you have this positive image of yourself and as you reflect a positive image of your own worth, then other people reflect that back to you. Isn't it true that if a person has that victim inside of themselves, if they feel that they're a victim, life seems to fall in on top of them and create victim and when you meet one of those people, it's almost as if you want to go punch him in the mouth just to keep them happy and they pool that to them. When you can see this image of yourself in this loving forgiveness, this unconditional love that you have for yourself, then it becomes simple to transfer that to outputs.

When a person is uncomfortable or frustrated or angry, what they're really saying is I'm angry with myself when they judge or criticize or Moan that judging and criticizing themselves. Because when you're sent and balanced and happy, you will see only happiness and beauty around you. And if somebody does something that you don't like and you are balanced, it won't affect her. And so only when you on balance and you don't have a strong idea of self image and self acceptance that you criticize all those, I need to express this negativity to the world and those people that you are negative to will react negatively back to you. And so the creative visualization process is to see you as this complete individual.

You haven't completed your journey, you're not perfect and that's perfect that you're not perfect. You can begin to put all that new energy and you can begin to look at your life. You avoid those areas that cause you emotional problems. I don't mean avoid in the sense of dodging them, but what I mean is you are careful not to be sucked into situations you know that you don't deal with. Well, you engineer your life to enhance the strengths, what I call race statues to your strengths and then eventually all the weaknesses fall away.

The next idea that I'd like to discuss in relation to creative visualization is for you to begin to visualize what your higher purpose in life is. To have a life that's just mundane, working and surviving and procreating and bringing up the kids and doing the washing up or whatever it is, is not alive of excitement. It doesn't have a high purpose and for you to visualize that highest purpose inside your feelings, it begins to give you something to go for. It gives you a higher ideal. Tend to cater to the fullest like dedication to the things that are truly wonderful in life and so that would be your next step. Once you have a powerful image that you can carry out to the world that can be some use to the world.

Then you're looking at developing a dedication, a higher purpose, and if you don't have a higher purpose and your feelings right now, then use creative visualization to see yourself walking in or walking through life with some kind of higher purpose, whatever that purpose may be though many possibilities open to you, perhaps a great diplomat, a peacemaker, perhaps suppose and of great creativity perhaps up us and who brings to life this incredible ability to nudge, to care for people. Perhaps you an organizer and that's your gift to the world and you can organize it. Perhaps you lead and you can lead it.

Page 60

Perhaps you are a supporter and you can attach
yourself to a leader and know and understand that
the supportive role is as important as the lead as
role. Perhaps you are a healer, then you can bring
a healing to yourself and put the people around
you, but each and all of us have something that we
can contribute. You'll give to the world is what
you are, and of course if you're happy with what
you are, your gift is a happy gift. Next, you may
want to consider using creative visualization for
goals. Secondly, and the whole trick to goal
setting is to not set goals that are impossible for
you because if you can conceptualize it in your
feelings or visualize it in your feelings, then that
goal will never be reached. And so I'm like goal
setting, which is only a little way in front of where
you are now.

And so everything is manageable and everything is possible and it isn't something where you're asking for the absolute impossible because they'll have things that are impossible to you right now given the total quantum of energy that is you. However, as you begin to grow from one goal to the next and you begin to expand your experience and your abilities in the physical plane, then other areas and other goals and other possibilities become real to you. The other thing about goals is of course that you have to have the ability to let them go, to release them. You're going to go for the goal. If it changes, change it. You don't have to be dogmatic. Isn't it true that when you see people that set out on some kind of quest in a very dogmatic way and they live 20 years in the desert looking for some type of little beetle or something, you often run that.

Why did they bother? Why didn't they see that off the one or two years in the desert looking for this beetle? It was a totally worthless way of spending their life. But what happens is we give the mind to task and it's almost like it fixes itself upon that task and I think it's important for you to be fluid and to change the goals whenever you need to. You can use creative visualization to see yourself through projects. If you have a project that you have to deliver at a certain time in a separate place or you have a creative idea, more than likely you're going to pull to you out the people that will help you make that project work.

And as you begin to pull other people to you, you have to understand that they will have all the own beliefs Sunday on understandings of what the project is and somehow you have to transfer to them what it is you want, how the project will be handled, how the thing will materialize. As you do that, you have to have a strong image of what is the project and creative visualization allows you to run through in your mind. It's a bit like a dress rehearsal, what you run through the project and you see it coming to its final glorious conclusion.

As you run through the project in a creative visualization process, you can not only look at any kinks and bumps and things that perhaps you may need to change in order for the project to be successful, but also you begin to infuse the project with light and positivity. It's almost as if the project is an idea in the mind of man, you are pulling to you other people. You have to create the project in Nan mind and all of you have to infuse the project in light. When you look at the physical plane, it is all materialization of full. If you look at a famous bridge that's a solid bridge, but it was originally and soulful and the thought form had to have light to type of positivity.

It had to have the ability to complete the project. It had to have fallen food financing and maybe a thousand people worked on putting that bridge together, but somebody somewhere was guiding that thing and granting everybody an idea of what the thought for me is, hey, this is the thoughtful, this amount of scaffolding, this amount of steel, this amount of concrete, this is how we'll hold the bridge up. This is how we're paid for it, and so when you go through creative visualization, you can infuse into your life this light that will allow these projects to take place.

It's particularly important, say in a business situation or in an office where you have to motivate other people and a whole group of you have to get together to materialize an action plan or a sales force or whatever it is that you're doing. As you begin to see all of those people responding positively to you, you can also begin to use creative visualization to see them understanding what the project is. Often when a project fails, it fails because of a lack of communication. People cannot read your mind. You will think that they automatically know what to feel and who you are and what you want.

They don't. And you can say to somebody, please dig a hole here and you presume they know what you mean. But inside the mind of the person listening to the instruction, they don't necessarily know and what they think is a hole here may be a totally different concept of what you think. Dig a hole him meetings and so they dig a little round hole that's a foot deep. And what you really wanted was an oak belonged trench 30 yards wide. And so if you understand that, if using creative visualization and becoming organized in your feelings, you get a very clear concept of what you want, then you can say to that person, I need a whole head. It needs to be 30 yards long, flee yards wide.

And it's going to go from the lamppost to the tree and everybody understands what you want. And usually you're going to have to find the, you're going to have to tell people three times before they really understand something. So later in the conversation you will say, by the way, do you know how long this hole is? They say, yep, 30 yachts. Okay, where's it going to be built? Then you go back and you say how wide the hole is? And they say, well, you want it as wide as a spade. And you guys say, Nope, I don't want as wide a spade. I want it three feet wide. And you begin to explain to people what you want.

And you can only do that if it's a conceptual idea, you know, feelings and that conceptualization of feelings has clarity. And so as you begin to use this process, you can see that what you're really doing is, is you're becoming organized and successful.

Page 70

Wealth Affirmation

It is very important that you say and belief in
these wealth affirmation.

1. I am a money magnet
2. I am an absolute money magnet
3. I love money. Money worships me!
4. Every day I am attracting more and more money
5. Money is welcome in my life.
6. My income exceeds my expenses

My middle name is money

7. I love money, money love me

8. Money is coming to me

9. I thank the universe for a lot of money that flows into me

10. I know what I want and expect in my life

11. I expect a large amount of money from unknown sources

12. I radiate vibrations of prosperity and wealth

13. I receive lots of money from the universe

14. Money flows in my life

15. I feel wealth flowing toward me now

I have an abundance of whatever I need

16. I am tuned into the flow of prosperity
17. The more money I spend, the more money I have and receive
18. Money constantly flows into my life
19. My life is full of abundance
20. I am aligned with the energy of wealth and abundance
21. I am simply wealthy
22. I always think positively about money and wealth
23. I have a money mindset
24. Attracting money is easy
25. I attract money continuously
26. Money comes to me easily and effortlessly
27. I am always grateful for sources of income

I am becoming richer every day.

28.I receive money just by thinking luxuriously

29.Unexpected money simply falls into my lap

30.I am a great success!

31.I love money!

32.My bank account is always growing

33.I am becoming rich

34.Every day I am becoming richer and richer

35.I am financially abundant

36.I success in everything I do

37.I am an unlimited being

38.I am created for wealth and abundance

39.Money comes to me naturally

40.My income is constantly increasing

41. I am a living money magnet

42. I prosper wherever I turn

43. I always attract money into my life

44. I am doing what I love and earning lots of money

45. I am worthy!

46. My wallet is bulging with money.

Reinforcing Your Money Affirmation

I can and will have more than I ever dreamed possible.

- I feel good about money and deserve it in my life.
- Great wealth is flowing to me now.
- I now create my wonderful, ideal life.
- I am thankful for the comfort and joy that money provides me.
- I know I am abundant.
- I always have enough money for myself.
- Every day in every way I am becoming more and more prosperous.
- I see myself as wealthy, and that's who I am.
- I choose wealth and abundance.

My wealth derives from honesty in everything I do.

- I am worthy of great success.
- My greatest good is coming to me now.
- I love abundance in all its beautiful forms.
- I am wide awake to my abundance.
- I release all my negative beliefs about money and invite wealth into my life.
- I am prosperous, healthy, happy and live in abundance.
- Wealth is my birth-right, my natural state of being.

- Making money is good for me and for everyone in my life.
- My income is growing higher and higher now.
- Money is an important part of my life and is never away from me.
- All my issues with wealth have disappeared.
- I clearly see opportunities to effortlessly make money.
- I am wealthy.
- Whatever I do, it always ends in amassing wealth.
- I attract prosperity.
- Money flows freely and abundantly into my life.
- I will be productive and prosperous today
- My prosperity is unlimited, my success is unlimited now.

- Every day in every way, my wealth is increasing.
- I am destined to find prosperity in everything I do.
- I am gracious for the wealth I have in my life.
- I am free to do whatever I wish to do.

Affirmations to Attract Money

- Today is filled with opportunity, and I will seize it.
- Being wealthy gives me joy, happiness and peace of mind.
- I am now free to do the things I love.
- Everything good is coming to me easily and effortlessly.
- Thank you Universe for my great abundance.

I allow all good things to come into my life, and I enjoy them.

- Wealth is a positive expression of divine energy.
- I can easily imagine myself having limitless abundance.
- Money always flows to me easily.
- I realize that I can help others with my wealth; so I stay wealthy.
- I am prosperous in everything I do.
- I am thankful for the abundance and prosperity in my life. Abundance around me, abundance within me, abundance throughout me.

- All my needs are met instantaneously.
- I know there is ample prosperity for all.
- I have the power to be successful.
- I allow my passions to perpetuate good in the world through my wealth.
- I let go of all resistance to prosperity, and it comes to me naturally.
- I am magnetic to money, and it is magnetic to me.
- Prosperity now happens to me.
- Money flows freely in my life.
- I am relaxing into greater abundance.
- I now release the goldmine within me.

I am worthy of receiving prosperity now. I am willing to be more abundant now.

- I am now accumulating large sums of money.
- Like a powerful magnet, I attract all my desires in great abundance.
- I release all opposition to wealth.
- I am certain that my path is always perfect for me.
- I am abundant.
- Abundance is my divine birthright.
- Prosperity and abundance surround me.
- I release all negativity around building wealth.
- I attract prosperity with each thought I think.
- I am extremely successful.
- I deserve the best and it comes to me now.

Affirmations To Attract Money

- There is plenty of money in the Universe, and there is plenty for me.
- My mind is constantly attracting money into my life.
- My mind is in harmony with the energies that create abundance.
- I am attracting into my life opportunities for making money.
- Each day, I am getting more comfortable about the idea of having a lot of money.
- I am getting used to the idea of being wealthy.
- I am confident that the Universe is helping me get all the money I need, and even more.

If other people achieved success, I can too.

- My bank manager always welcomes me with a big smile.
- Piles of money are piling up in my bank account.
- I have a great job with a wonderful salary.
- My financial situation is improving beyond my dreams.
- My business is attracting a lot of paying customers.
- Money is appearing in my life through many channels, and in harmonious ways.

Wealth Affirmations

- You don't want to – you're perfectly happy with your state of finances.
- You don't think you deserve it even though you'd never admit this.
- You don't think it's possible given your life's situation.
- You think rich is evil and poverty is noble.
- You think money will make you do bad things.
- You feel torn, guilty and conflicted about your desire to be wealthy and prosperous.
- You blame your parents for not having enough money and not teaching you better.
- You believe riches are bestowed upon a lucky few.

You think you will be unhappy because money isn't supposed to buy happiness.

- You think the only way to be wealthy is if you married into wealth or came of wealth.
- You have none of these self-limiting beliefs; you just have no idea how to make more money yet you won't seek expert advice.

Money Affirmation Repetition

I have more than enough money.

I encourage everyone around me to be healthy.

Money flows to me.

I embrace new avenues of income.

I recognize and embrace wealth building opportunities.

Every day I am attracting and saving more money.

I choose wealth and abundance.

I use money to build my best life.

Prosperity of every kind is drawn toward me.

I constantly attract opportunities that create more money.

I attract wealth.

Money comes to me in expected and unexpected ways.

I release all negative energy over money.

I am open and receptive to all the wealth that life offers me.

My actions create prosperity.

I welcome an unlimited supply of income and wealth in my life.

I move from poverty thinking to abundance thinking.

Money comes to me effortlessly, easily, and frequently.

I am a magnet for money.

I am worthy of making more money.

Wealth constantly flows in my life.

I am the master of my wealth.

Money expands my life's opportunities and experiences.

I use money to help others.

Money creates a positive impact on my life.

I am surrounded by abundance.

I am able to achieve whatever I desire.

My life is full of prosperity.

I deserve prosperity and abundance.

I am at peace with having a lot of money.

My income is more than exceeds my expenses.

I know what I want and expect in my life.

The more I spend, the more I have and receive.

I am always grateful for sources of income.

My bank account is always growing.

I am financially abundant.

I am created for wealth and abundance.

Everything is going to work out for my highest good.

I am doing what I love and earning lots of money.

I am worthy!

Remember

Belief is the

Keys to

Manifesting Wealth!

Acting and feeling like you are

Already Successful and Wealthy

Are also the keys to

Manifesting Wealth.

Good Luck to Quest

and

Journey to Manifesting Wealth

Copyright Material

The Keys to

Success and

Wealth

Law of Attraction

By, Arsenio Pelayo

www.ingramcontent.com/pod-product-compliance
Lightning Source LLC
Chambersburg PA
CBHW021849170526
45157CB00007B/3005